QUOTES PLUS:

A BOOK OF QUOTES & THOUGHTS
OF A DEEP THINKER PLUS TRUE SHORT STORIES

WRITTEN BY DR. NEENAH BOYD, PHD-HNSD

COVER DESIGN & PHOTOS BY WILLIAM BOYD

DORRANCE
PUBLISHING CO
EST. 1920
PITTSBURGH, PENNSYLVANIA 15238

The contents of this work, including, but not limited to, the accuracy of events, people, and places depicted; opinions expressed; permission to use previously published materials included; and any advice given or actions advocated are solely the responsibility of the author, who assumes all liability for said work and indemnifies the publisher against any claims stemming from publication of the work.

Dorrance Publishing Co
585 Alpha Drive
Pittsburgh, PA 15238
Visit our website at *www.dorrancebookstore.com*

ISBN: 978-1-6386-7012-4
ESIBN: 978-1-6386-7961-5

QUOTES PLUS:

A BOOK OF QUOTES & THOUGHTS
OF A DEEP THINKER PLUS TRUE SHORT STORIES

TABLE OF CONTENTS

ACKNOWLEDGMENTS

I want to thank my modest yet communicative best friend and husband, **William Boyd**, for believing in me and making it known to me that he is proud of me. He helped me talk out my thoughts and analyze aspects of my life that are reflected in my writing. He spent his precious time proofreading, critiquing, and reading for pleasure each section of this book. I am also thankful for his cover design and photography in the true short story of the Ark Encounter. It was his spirituality that led us to visit it in Kentucky, USA.

I want to thank my daughter **Tammy Ramsey-Gordon** and her husband **Eric Gordon** for their Godly influence on me, which always pointed me in the direction to use my gifts even in my retirement. I carry their closeness to me in proximity as well as in my heart as a high honor.

I want to thank my friend, **Rabbi Mark Mahler**, Rabbi Emeritus of Temple Emanuel in the South Hills of Pittsburgh, Pennsylvania, who often expressed delight in my quotes and said he was going to quote me. Mark graduated cum laude and gives my theological muscles a healthy workout as we email back and forth deep thoughts and insights.

I want to thank my friend and so much more, **Minister Etasha Arnold**, a manager at NASA in California, and preacher at Shining Light

Worship Center, to whom I taught Beginner's Hebrew. She heard three of my quotes and said they were, "pearls!" She motivated me to get them published through Dorrance Publishing Company, Inc.

I want to acknowledge **Emily Harris** from the Woman2Woman Toastmasters International Club in Squirrel Hill in Pittsburgh, Pennsylvania who wanted to know the backstory of how I got a thank-you letter from His Royal Highness, Prince Charles of Wales. Emily's curiosity was the incentive for me to write that true story.

I want to acknowledge **Peter Hart, Jr.,** my friend and SCORE business mentor, graduate of MIT and Harvard, who also took his family to see the Ark Encounter. Pete is a super strong encourager and helped me keep the momentum going to reach the success of getting my book published.

I want to thank all of the people who helped me iron out sections of this book, or who were a blessing to me in many other ways; namely all of my relatives, including but not limited to my sisters **Deborah Rankin** and **Edwina L. Kaikai**, **Barbara Rooks** and **Karen Haynes** and niece **Christina Kaikai**; current and lifelong friends, including but not limited to **Bernita Webb-Jones** and **Denise Allen**; friends and instructors from my class at Chatham University's Center for Women's Entrepreneurship, including but not limited to **Claire Linderman**, **Tiffany Ward**, **Kate Davis Booker**, and **Beth Sanchez**; and the wonderful staff at Dorrance Publishing Company, Inc. including but not limited to, **LaSheri Walls, Madalyn Whitaker,** and **David Zeolla**.

I could not have gotten this far in my authorship without all of you. If anyone feels that I left them out, please charge it to my head and not my heart.

DEDICATIONS

This book is dedicated to my mother and father,
who were the perfect married couple that
loved each other and raised me with
the security and confidence that
comes with being loved.

This book is also dedicated to my
intelligent husband, William Boyd,
whose loyal love for me aroused
my inner strength to persevere
and complete this book.

ABOUT THE BOOK

QUOTES PLUS: The Book of Quotes & Thoughts of a Deep Thinker plus True Short Stories:
Quotes are a dime a dozen. They uplift, inspire, and encourage. They change a person's perspectives and enlighten. Reading a quote can affirm previous thoughts or offer a new look at a situation. Some quotes can have an opposite effect that disproves a previous thought... which can be healthy.

Each quote or thought in this collection has a companion quote or thought on the next line. Some are brief, memorable, and easily quotable. Two true short stories follow the quotes and thoughts. One is about a thank-you letter to me sent by His Royal Highness, Prince Charles of Wales. The other is about the replica of Noah's Ark in Kentucky, USA.

The entire book of quotes, thoughts, and short stories are originals and come from my depth of education, professional life as a Speech/Language Pathologist for 30 years in the schools with my niche with gifted junior high students, extensive Jewish and Christian theology, practice of the 613 commandments, and leadership thereof; as well as business world experience as the Founder, CEO/CFO of a humanitarian nonprofit, and roles in Toastmasters International, which is the organization that helps adults improve their public speaking and leadership skills. There, I had the roles as Vice President of Education, Area Director, and briefly the role of Vice President of Membership.

It is because of my long career, education, and life's experiences that I have seen the heights people can reach. As a deep thinker, I attempt to give that extra bit of motivation a person needs to be more successful in whatever area in their lives that they want more direction and self-discipline. I believe everyone can be more successful than they are with the right tools and inspiration. The short stories are loaded with inspiration that will leave the reader highly encouraged.

This book was written so that the contents would be widely quoted, shared, given as gifts, used to bolster articles, research papers, etc. Cover design and photos were done by my fantastic husband and my greatest supporter, William Boyd.

ON WORKERS. ON LEADERSHIP:

1. Remember,
   Those unsure, **MIGHT** complete a given task.
   Those that can, **WILL** complete a given task.
   Those that do, **DO** complete a given task.
2. **There are all types of workers. As a leader, encourage and reassure all of them according to their level of output. Believe in them all!**

ON TEAMS:

3. A lazy team member can pull a whole team down.
4. **Lazy team member? Team collapses.**

ON TEAMS:

5. An argumentative team member can move a stalling team into discovery, then they can pivot.
6. **Argumentative team member? Team excels.**

ON HOPE:

7. Hope, is knowing that He can.
    Faith, is knowing that He will.
    Joy, is knowing that He can and will.
    Happiness, is knowing that He could and did.
    Peace, is knowing and understanding all of this.
8. **He can make it happen!**

ON LOVE:

9. I may not be able to love you completely; but I completely desire to love you forever.
10. **Try love.**

ON INTELLIGENCE. ON KINDNESS.

11. The smarter you are, the kinder you become. Because, if you're not kind, then you're not smart.
12. **Intelligence begets kindness!**

ON GOD:

13. Have God on your Business Team.
14. **For God is a businessman.**

ON GRAY DAYS:

15. Smell the rain and fragrance of flowers.

16. Rainy days make sweet smelling flowers grow and deep thinkers blossom.

ON TIME MANAGEMENT. A LIFE LINE:

17. Traditional American schooling lasts 13 years from kindergarten until a senior in high school graduates.

If you retire at age 66 and live till you're 86, that's 20 years. Which is longer, mandatory schooling or retirement?

18. Don't waste the precious time you're in school. It's short. Retirement may be longer. Where will you get the money to buy a car when you're retired, or buy food or clothes? Be sure to learn good social skills and communication skills so that you're the type of person that gets along with everyone. You may end up living with family members that you'd rather not live with, but have to due to health reasons or lack of money to live on your own when you grow old. Kids begin to learn social skills in the home from ages 0–5 years old. They play with their brothers and sisters and learn to respect their parents and older people, among other things that they learn before entering kindergarten. Then it is important to talk nicely to your classmates, teachers, and school staff during your school-age days. Social skills should develop to the point that when you graduate from high school you are well adjusted and able to get along with your employees if you're the boss, your boss if not, your coworkers, sergeant or captain if you go into the

military, or those at the college you may attend, or your spouse if you get married.

You want to learn to get along with family members, children, cousins, aunts, uncles, stepparents, half brothers and half sisters, etc. You may end up having to live with them, or in a facility with others. Conduct grades in school, or what used to be called "Citizenship" grades are just as important as, or even more so, than subject grades like math, science, and reading. Learning to talk a certain way, so that you don't get into fights or arguments, likely increases your chances of living a peaceful life with less stress. It also likely increases the chances that you don't live with loneliness and sleeplessness. Having restful nights when you lie down to sleep is important for good health.

19. **On a Funny Note. Mild Earthquake:**
   What did the Earth say to the people after a mild earthquake?

20. **Oops, my fault.**

* I survived two Californian earthquakes. One registered a magnitude of 7.2 on the Richter scale. I was 200 miles from the epicenter. I will never forget the sound of the rumble and roar, and the sensation under my feet of the earth quaking.

ON PERSEVERANCE:

21. Let a rest period be a part of your attempts towards success.

22. **Try, Try, Try, Rest, Try again.**

ON PERSEVERANCE:

23. Even when it takes longer to do, pay attention to details.
24. **Don't be lazy!**

ON TEASING:

25. Even when playful and humorous teasing happens, someone walks away hurt.
26. **Teasing hurts inside.**

ON PARENTING:

27. Be a giver of praise. Psychological wages pay well.
28. **Make each child feel like your favorite.**

ON SUCCESS AND SELF-DISCIPLINE:

29. Prove that you function and operate in a methodical, disciplined, above board, honest fashion.
30. **Fastidious attention to details pays off!**

ON TRUST:

31. The Bible says, happy is the person who trusts God.
32. **I say, happier is the person that God trusts.**

ON GIVING LOVE:

33. Why are some people so loving? Maybe they were loved a lot as a child.
34. **He who is loved much, loves much.**

ON PEACE:

35. When your inners are quiet and still, and you're like a plant or tree; free and at peace you will be.
36. **Rejoice in your still life and believe in yourself.**

A LETTER FROM A PRINCE
HIS ROYAL HIGHNESS, PRINCE CHARLES OF WALES

by Dr. Neenah Boyd, PhD-HNsD
Retired Speech/Language Pathologist

All schools want to have high-achieving students…students who eagerly do extra-credit work or go the extra mile on their own…students who ask questions that challenge the teachers. Not every school was like that during my career, but some were. I observed what made a school great and took those techniques to every school that I serviced.

The Principal at Willow Orchard Jr. High School in Contin, New Mexico, USA* addressed the teachers at a staff meeting with a confrontational opening. He said, "If you're the type of teacher that arrives to work when the late bell rings at 7:10 A.M., and leaves as soon as the dismissal bell rings at 1:25 P.M., you're on survival. You're not in it for the kids." Sadly, Willow Orchard Jr. High was a low-achieving school.

The Principal then challenged the teachers to come up with some way to raise the academic achievement level of the student body. Knowing that was a large undertaking, I thought in my mind, "How can I help and participate in this worthy venture?" Most Speech/Language Pathologists would not even attend a teachers' staff meeting in the first place, or not to mention, think that the challenge applied to them. But I wanted to help. I was a different type of Speech/Language Pathologist. I worked with courtesy and integrity, giving my all to what I felt

God led me there to do, drawing on all of my education, experience with high-achieving schools, and mostly allowing my caring, God-led heart to lead the way. I would arrive in the morning when the custodian unlocked the doors at 6:30 A.M. and did not usually leave till 3:30 P.M. There was another junior high principal who called me a "Speech Pathologist extraordinaire." Could I really pull off this teacher challenge, though?

Prince Charles wrote me a flattering thank-you letter, stating that I am kind and generous. But what prompted His Royal Highness to send me the letter? It was Rose Marie*, a student of mine working on the "R" sound which effected how she said words like, "bird", "robot," "rear," and.........."Rose Marie."

I decided I would challenge my students to give an oral report on an extra-credit project. The thought of the extra-credit project electrified me! I had Speech Students who saw me to improve their communication skills in the areas of stuttering, voice disorders, articulation of troublesome consonants and vowels, understanding and expressing thoughts, and interacting verbally, any of which effected their participation and achievement in class. They had to research the topic of the extra credit project and present their findings in an oral report using good speech and language communication skills. Doing so would win them an Etch-A-Sketch, which I displayed on the chalkboard ledge as an incentive. But I really wanted my students to want to do the extra-credit project regardless of the prize. After all, they were 7th and 8th graders, mature enough to do it because of inner inspiration.

I hastened to the school library to get the librarian ready for an onslaught of eager speech students to look up the difference between a toad and a frog. Thinking that would be an easy extra-credit project, I excitedly told my students the project and waited to hear the oral reports. Time passed. More time passed. No one came forward. But I did not give up on my students. I gave them a second chance.

The new project was to report on which lives longer…the caterpillar or the butterfly? I even asked them what teacher on campus could they ask to get the answer. No one did this either. Was I ready to give up on these students and resolve that this school just had very low-functioning children uninterested in school and learning? No, I was not ready to give up on them.

A glimmer of hope arose during a therapy session. We were playing Spanish Bingo as reinforcement. They had to match shapes and colors spoken by me in Spanish, after they used an [s] sound correctly in a sentence, or spoke for 30 seconds without stuttering, or whatever target skill was on their IEP (Individual Education Plan) that they needed to work on. When we came to a brown rectangle, I said, "Rectangulo marron" for brown rectangle. My students shouted, "No! Café!, trying to correct my translation of "brown." I said, "No, marron." They argued with me thinking of the common use of "café" for a shade of brown that looks like coffee with milk. My Assistant who was from Ecuador, South America and spoke Spanish as her native language, remained silent during the verbal battle back and forth, giving deference to me since she knew that I learned Spanish from my high school Spanish teacher who was from Spain…the motherland. The next day Angela Martinez,* a student that was a handful to handle and a frequent behavior problem with other teachers in her other classes, told the group that her grandmother told her that "marron" means "dark brown," which was the shade of brown on the card.

I held my chest and gasped by what Angela said. She actually conveyed that she talked about school at home. She discussed Speech Class and enlisted her grandmother's help. That's the kind of student I wanted Willow Orchard Jr. High to have. So thrilled and encouraged, I gave Angela a Magic Doodle Board for going the extra mile.

I then gave my students another chance to do an extra-credit project and oral report. (Sigh) I cleared my throat and said softly in an audible voice to myself, "I still believe in them."

The first extra-credit project that I gave them, that required them to utilize the books and encyclopedias in the school library, gave me an idea for a third and ultimately last project. You may think that all they needed to do is do a Google search for the answer. But the principal's teachers challenge came during the 2001-2002 school year. Cell phones weren't widely used by junior high students and flat screen computer monitors weren't either. Students were still using World Book and Britannica encyclopedias.

Not too long before that, I had purchased my own set of Encyclopedia Britannica. I proudly told my students this and informed them that I received a free book with my purchase which I read with great enjoyment. The book was entitled, *Royal Service*. It was about the life of Prince Charles spanning twelve years up to the age when he was involved with Princess Diana.

For the extra-credit project, I told my students that Prince Charles has good communication skills as he meets and greets people from all different countries. In letting the children know that Prince Charles has to wear a particular and different dignified outfit for each country he visits, I told them that he didn't have to figure out which outfit to wear each time. He had a servant-valet that did that. It was the valet that wrote the book, *Royal Service*. For the extra-credit project, the only thing that the students had to do was tell me the author's name of *Royal Service*, and use good speech and language skills in doing so. Both weary and excited about giving my students another opportunity to increase their educational prowess, I even made it easy on them. I told them that one of his names is Barry.

Time passed. Then…in a mad rush…Rose Marie, a seventh-grade student working on her articulation of the [r] sound, burst into my room early in the morning with the excitement of a lottery winner!!! "Mrs. Granger,"* she said with perfect [r] sounds. She continued, "I know the author of *Royal Service*!!!" Smiling and beaming, she proudly said, Stephen P. Barry!!!" Rose Marie said all of this with good [r] sounds. She was exactly right! She ended her oral report by asking if she can have the Etch-A-Sketch then or if she had to wait till her speech therapy time. Of course, I said she could take it then.

Rose Marie said her father took her to their local library to solve the project problem. I was pleased with the extra steps this student did on her own. She talked about Speech Class at home and motivated her father to be involved in her education. Hooray!! I was overjoyed and wrote to His Royal Highness, Prince Charles of Wales, to let him know that I used him as a role model for my students as one who has good communication skills, not thinking in any way that he would reply. But he did. He thanked me.

I wrote my letter to Prince Charles over a weekend. As I sat satisfied with my wording, phraseology, punctuation and all, I pondered how I was going to get his address. I thought I could call Buckingham Palace's information line and get it from there. I got the phone number and dialed. The phone rang and rang. I thought I would get an automated greeting and a prompt to the address. That did not happen. Well, sort of it did. A recorded male voice which was very deep, loud, and threatening, came on and said, "You have reached the Royal Palace. If you do not have a good reason to call the Royal Palace, Hang. Up. Now!" That was intimidating, but I waited for the prompt to get the address. That did not happen. A live man with a mellow voice came on the line and said questioningly, "Hello?" Startled, I stumbled over my words and told him what I did with my Speech students and that I wanted to let Prince Charles know that I used him as a role model for them. I asked the guard if he knows Stephen P. Barry. He told me, yes, and that he had passed away. We shared a moment of silence respectfully. Then the mood turned lighthearted and comical as he gave me the address.

About a month later, it was a regular day at Willow Orchard Jr. High. I was seeing the students on my caseload as usual. My Assistant went to the office to get my mail as she usually did in the morning. Doing therapy with my students, I was unaware that she had left the room and had come back. She came back quietly and sat at her desk holding the letter from Buckingham Palace and waited for the perfect time to let me know that His Royal Highness, Prince Charles of Wales had written me back.

After the speech therapy group had gone, my Assistant said, "I got your mail" and handed it to me. I set all of the mail aside not noticing the heavy envelope from London. My Assistant didn't say anything further.

I continued with my day of doing therapy with groups of adolescents with their problems of stuttering, articulation, voice, and language disorders that I tried to ameliorate or bring to extinction. I ignored the mail which I had a proclivity of doing. The students were coming in and out my Speech Class as usual. When my Lunch/Prep Period came, I went about the task of opening my mail. My eyes grew big and a giant smile crossed my lips when I saw "THE ENVELOPE," as my Assistant watched me. Both of us broke out with laughter and cheered with excitement!!

I didn't open the envelope for days. I couldn't open it. I was so filled with emotion. A weekend passed. The envelope was so heavy that I thought it contained tickets to tour Buckingham Palace that he was sending to my student who solved the extra-credit project. But it was not. It was the kind letter to me on royal stationery, where he thanked me and called me both kind and generous.

I wrote up a news release for the Morning Announcements at Willow Orchard stating that Mrs. Granger's lively and exciting Speech Class heard from Buckingham Palace in London because of Rose Marie Thompson, and so forth. This piqued Rose Marie's Special Ed teacher. Yes, Rose Marie was in the lowest Special Ed classroom on campus for intellectually disabled students. Her teacher told me that Rose Marie was doing very well in her classroom too and had the school psychologist reevaluate her. He did and found that she no longer belonged in that Special Ed classroom, something quite unheard of. She was assigned to a Resource Teacher and given General Ed classes where she made "Bs" and "Cs."

This story is not just about the greatest letter ever written to me. It's about moments of being inspired…on multiple levels. The Principal inspired me. I inspired my students. Rose Marie inspired her father. The story inspired Prince Charles, Rose Marie's teacher, the school psychologist, and others in between, proving that you CAN raise academic functioning, one student, one father, one teacher, one school psychologist, one Prince, and one Speech Pathologist extraordinaire at a time!

*Names of all people and places were changed for privacy protection where appropriate.

Dr. Neenah Boyd is a woman of faith. She is married to William Boyd, a former hospital supervisor with a degree in Fine Arts. They met online in 2010 in different cities, different states, different time zones. She is pictured in her husband's TV show T-shirt, "Touched by an Angel," that he wore while driving alone, the 600-mile journey from his hometown to marry her three years later. They have four children between them with six grandchildren, and a son in Heaven at age 34. Neenah graduated from the G. D. Carmile Private School of Theology & Philosophy, receiving her spiritual doctoral degree, PhD-HNsD, which is a cross between a degree in theology and neurospirituology. Tested at age 11, Neenah has a high IQ. When she was in junior high, her father wanted her to join Mensa, the high IQ society. She battled racism in graduate school, but completed her medical speech/language pathology hospital practicum as well as clinical and Master's degree theory from the University of Pittsburgh. She also received a degree in Education and Communication Sciences and Disorders from Indiana University of Pennsylvania. Neenah was dedicated to her 30-year career as a Speech/Language Pathologist in the schools, highlighted by a thank-you letter from His Royal Highness, Prince Charles of Wales. Neenah has private practice experience with two adult clients and is an author doing postdoctoral studies in neurospirituology and theology. photo by Eric Gordon

MY IMPRESSIONS OF OUR TRIP TO THE ARK ENCOUNTER

written by Dr. Neenah Boyd, PhD-HNsD
photos by William Boyd
(Except where indicated)

A trip to Kentucky sounded odd to me until my husband told me why he wanted to go. He was doing a detailed study of the Bible starting in the book of Genesis and thought that seeing the replica of Noah's Ark would be enlightening. Oh, it was. Was it ever!!! I wasn't warm to the idea at first for several good reasons in my opinion. But he REALLY wanted to go, which means a lot to me. Therefore, I watched a couple of YouTube videos on the subject and realized the extent of walking that would be done. Panic set in. I became awash with anxiety over the suspected hardship such an experience of walking and eyeing the museum-like Ark would place on my husband's arthritic knee. I imagined getting partway through the 3-tiered structure the length of about somewhat less than two football fields, and having to leave him and go scout out a wheelchair so that he could see the rest of the fantastic exhibits.

But that was not the case. Then what do you think happened? We spent 5 hours walking and resting on benches as my Godly prayerful husband and I enjoyed our Ark Encounter tremendously. Hubby prayed that I would go AND enjoy myself. God blessed us with health in his knee which gave him no problem the whole time. My anxiety left and was replaced with joyful anticipation. It is a blessing all due to my husband's fervent praying!!!

What impressed me the most? That was a question posed to us at the end of our stay by a staff member there. I was speechless, encumbered by a boatload of positive, impressionable vignettes running through my mind. I was unable to sort the awe-inspiring parts of the day and talk about them on that same day. Only God could help me process all that we saw and took in. It took me 10 days from our return home, to be able to write feedback to Kentucky on my impression of the Ark Encounter.

The Ark was huge and unlike the shape it is usually depicted in illustrations. It was long and also narrow. This did not surprise me owing to the fact that I saw it on YouTube. Furthermore, about 20 years ago I drew the Ark according to the cubit dimensions given to Noah by God in the Bible; however, I drew it scaled to fit my paper. It too turned out long and narrow to my surprise and initial disbelief.

It wasn't the magnitude and construct of the Ark as a whole that impressed me the most. It was the pillars that separated the three levels of the interior of the Ark. These pillars were made of unimaginably huge tree trunks. It took me to a mental place wondering how the cedar from Lebanon was transported to build the Temple in Jerusalem in biblical times. What a work of God!!! How was that done in Kentucky? It left me awestruck!!!

We saw two short films in the theater area of the second floor that gave a cinematic perspective of the building of the Ark and the ensuing Flood and the need to have a relationship with God. The lifelike mannequins moved, and lordy lordy, they talked! Plus, the few live animals there added a realness that you could feel as we strolled and read descriptions of the many, many exhibits. It took me to a mental place to ask myself what I would do for roughly 377 days on the Ark weathering the rain and waiting for the water to recede. I would prayerfully talk with God, write in my journal, talk to the other passengers, write to them, and listen to others tell their side of the God story they had, were having then, and hopes they were going to experience once on dry land again. I would build closer relationships with the other occupants on the Ark...animals included.

I was truly impressed with this must-see Ark Encounter.

PHOTO BY NEENAH BOYD
BILL AND NOAH'S ARK REPLICA

NEENAH AT THE BOW OF NOAH'S ARK REPLICA

THESE LLAMAS ARE ALIVE AND ATE OUT OF VISITORS' HANDS
INSIDE THE NOAH'S ARK ENCOUNTER.

MASSIVE!!!

William and Neenah Boyd are a married couple who met online in 2010. They were both on Black People Meet.com but did not find each other there. God brought them together on Black Christian People Meet.com and they married three years later. William has a history of attending private schools through college and earned his Fine Arts degree from Maryville University. Neenah received her spiritual doctoral degree, PhD-HNsD, which is a cross between a degree in theology and neurospirituology, from the G. D. Carmile Private School of Theology & Philosophy. Neenah has a high IQ. Her father wanted her to join Mensa, the high IQ society. She battled racism in graduate school, but completed her medical speech/language pathology hospital practicum as well as clinical and Master's degree theory from the University of Pittsburgh. She also received a degree in Education and Communication Sciences and Disorders from Indiana University of Pennsylvania. Neenah was dedicated to her 30-year career as a Speech/Language Pathologist in the schools, highlighted by a thank you letter from His Royal Highness, Prince Charles of Wales. Neenah has private practice experience with two adult clients and now is an author doing postdoctoral studies in neurospirituology and theology.

PHOTO BY NEENAH BOYD

CPSIA information can be obtained
at www.ICGtesting.com
Printed in the USA
BVHW020753010222
627178BV00006B/65/J